Vol. 2142

BEETHOVEN: EASIEST PIANO PIECES

44 Bagatelles, German Dances, Ländler, Minuets, Sonatinas, and more

ISBN 978-1-5400-3969-9

G. SCHIRMER, *Inc.*

DISTRIBUTED BY

7777 W. BLUEMOUND RD. P.O. BOX 13819 MILWAUKEE, WI 53213

www.schirmer.com
www.halleonard.com

CONTENTS

ALLEGRETTO
in B minor

Ludwig van Beethoven
WoO 61

BAGATELLE
in G minor

Ludwig van Beethoven
Op. 119, No. 1

mf
cresc.
dim.
p
sf
sf cresc.
f
legato
cresc.
dim.
pp

BAGATELLE

in A Major

Ludwig van Beethoven
Op. 119, No. 4

BAGATELLE
in C Major
Ludwig van Beethoven
Op. 119, No. 8
Moderato cantabile
p molto legato
cresc.
dim.
p
p cresc.
BAGATELLE
in A minor
Ludwig van Beethoven
Op. 119, No. 9
Vivace moderato
p
f
mf

BAGATELLE
in B-flat Major

Ludwig van Beethoven
Op. 119, No. 11

BAGATELLE
in C Major
"Lustig und Traurig"

Ludwig van Beethoven
WoO 54

BAGATELLE
in B-flat Major

Ludwig van Beethoven
WoO 60

BAGATELLE

in A minor
"Für Elise"

Ludwig van Beethoven
WoO 59

*Alternately:

* *Other versions have:

* * *Other editions:

ÉCOSSAISE
in G Major

Ludwig van Beethoven
WoO 23

ÉCOSSAISE
in E-flat Major

Ludwig van Beethoven
WoO 86

WALTZ
in D Major

Ludwig van Beethoven
WoO 85

GERMAN DANCE
in E-flat Major

Ludwig van Beethoven
WoO 8, No. 5

GERMAN DANCE
in G Major

Ludwig van Beethoven
WoO 8, No. 6

GERMAN DANCE

in C Major

Ludwig van Beethoven
WoO 8, No. 7

Trio

GERMAN DANCE
in D Major

Ludwig van Beethoven
WoO 13, No. 1

GERMAN DANCE
in B-flat Major

Ludwig van Beethoven
WoO 13, No. 2

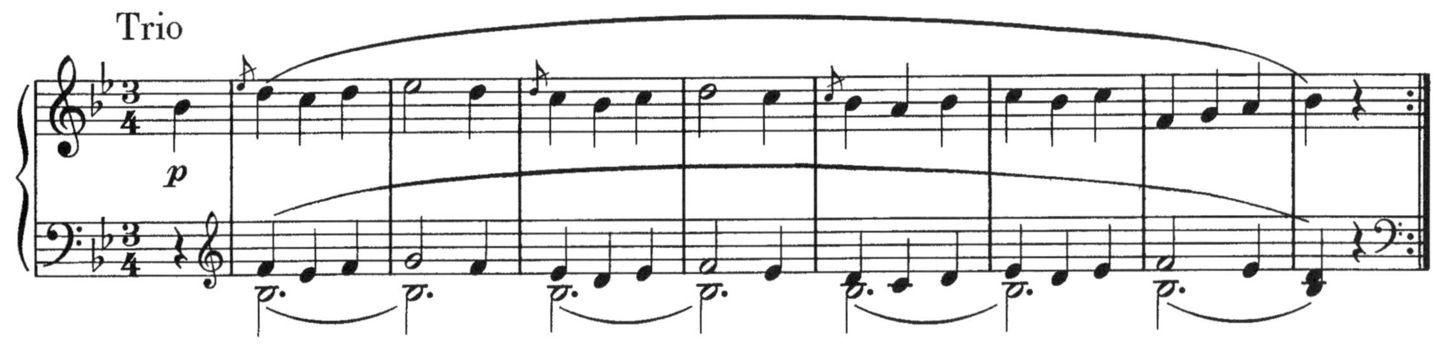

GERMAN DANCE
in B-flat Major

Ludwig van Beethoven
WoO 13, No. 6

GERMAN DANCE

in E-flat Major

Ludwig van Beethoven
WoO 13, No. 9

GERMAN DANCE
in C Major
Ludwig van Beethoven
WoO 13, No. 10
f
fz
fz
fz
fz
Fine
Trio
dolce
D.C.

SIX LÄNDLER

Ludwig van Beethoven
WoO 15

3

sf *sf* *sf* *sf*

4

* Alternate version:

**

5
sf 3
sf 3
sf 3
sf 3
sf 3
sf 3
sf 3
sf 3
sf 3
sf 3
sf 3
sf 3
sf 3
3
3
3
6
p
f

Coda

SEVEN LÄNDLER

Ludwig van Beethoven
WoO 11

mf
3
mf
p
mf
p
1.
2.

4
5

6
f
legato
p
f
f
p
7
sf
p
sf
p
sf

CODA
cresc.
f
p
cresc.
sf
cresc.
f

MINUET
in B-flat Major

Ludwig van Beethoven
WoO 7, No. 8

MINUET
in F Major

Ludwig van Beethoven
WoO 7, No. 12

MINUET
in G Major
Ludwig van Beethoven
WoO 10, No. 2
p
f
sf
1.
2.
Fine
Trio
D. C.

MINUET
in E-flat Major

Ludwig van Beethoven
WoO 10, No. 3

MINUET
in C Major
Ludwig van Beethoven
WoO 10, No. 6
sf
Fine
Trio
f
sf
sf
sf
sf
sf
sf
sf
ff
D.C.

MINUET
in E-flat Major

Ludwig van Beethoven
WoO 82

Trio
p
cresc.
p
cresc.
f
p
cresc.
Minuetto da capo

SONATA
in G minor

Edited and fingered by
Sigmund Lebert and Hans von Bülow

Ludwig van Beethoven
Op. 49, No. 1

Abbreviations: M. T., signifies Main Theme; S. T., Sub Theme; Cl. T., Closing Theme; D. G., Development-group; R., Return; Tr., Transition; Md. T., Mid-Theme; Ep., Episode; App., Appendix.

a) *mfp* signifies: the first note *mf*, the following ones *p*.

b) With the comma we indicate places where the player must perceptibly mark the end of a rhythmic group or section, by lifting the last note just before its time-value expires, although the composer wrote no rest.

c)

d) The left hand more subdued than the right, but still accenting the first of each pair of 16th-notes (i. e.: the bass notes proper) somewhat more than the second.

e)

f) Here and in the next measure the left hand should accent only the first note in each group of 16th-notes somewhat more than the others, but in all cases less than the soprano.

g) As at d.)

h) In these three measures as at f.)

a) As at (f) on the preceding Page.

b)

c) The left hand here again more subdued than the right.

d) As at (a).

e) In these twelve measures the first and third notes in each group of 16th notes should be made somewhat more prominent than the other notes, yet always in subordination to the melody, excepting the tones marked >

a) From here through the next 6 measures the left hand, having the melody, should predominate over the right, and, where it has 2 tones, chiefly accentuate the higher one.

b) As on first Page.

c) The next 5 measures as on first Page.

d) Doubtless literally meant neither for [music notation] nor for: [music notation] but [music notation]

e) This and the following turns again as on first Page.

f) From here onward as on second Page.

a)

b) Proceed only after a rest.

a) In these groups of 16th-notes, accent each first note slightly more than the 5 following, while subordinating all to the soprano. These same accented notes, too, (except in the fourth measure) should be held down during the second 16th-note.

b) Also subordinate this accompaniment, but accent the first note of each triplet, as the bass note proper, a trifle more than the other two.

a)

b) Here, of course, only the first eighth-note in each measure should be accented.

M. T
p
sf
cresc.
poco rit.
a tempo
p
cresc.
Tr.
p
f
p
f
S. T.
p dolce
p
p

a) From here up to the *ff* discreetly subordinate the left hand throughout (also in the repetitions of the fundamental tone.)

b) Let the *ff* enter abruptly with the fourth eighth-note, without any previous *crescendo*.

SONATA
in G Major

Edited and fingered by
Sigmund Lebert and Hans von Bülow

Ludwig van Beethoven
Op. 49, No. 2

Abbreviations: M.T. signifies Main Theme; S.T., Sub-Theme; Cl. T., Closing Theme; D.G., Development-Group; R., Return; Tr., Transition; Md. T. Mid-Theme; Ep., Episode.

a) Strike all short appoggiaturas on the beat, simultaneously with the accompaniment-note.

b) F♯ should be executed as a long, accented appoggiatura:

D. G.
M. T.
Ep.
cresc.
a)

S. T.
cresc.
p
Ep.
f
mf
a)
tr
sf
a) easier:

a) *mp* (*mezzo piano*, moderately soft) signifies a degree of tone-power midway between *p* and *mf*.

S. T. I.
cresc.
f
p
p
poco rit.
pp

M.T.
a tempo.
p
mp
cresc.
S.T.II.
f
cresc.
f dimin.

M. T.
pp
p
cresc.
mp
cresc.
f
Coda.
p
p
mf
cresc.
f
poco rit.
pp

SONATINA
in G Major

Ludwig van Beethoven
Anh. 5, No. 1

ROMANZE

SONATINA
in F Major

Ludwig van Beethoven
Anh. 5, No. 2

f
p
f
p
f
dim.
p
f
dolce

cresc.
RONDO
Allegro

ad libitum
a tempo
p
mf
p
mf
p
f

WALTZ
in E-flat Major

Ludwig van Beethoven
WoO 84

Trio

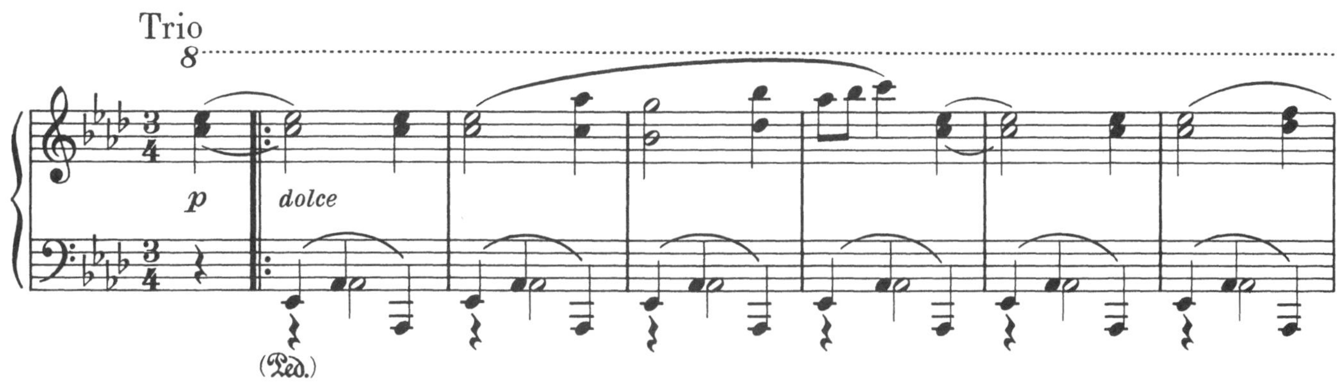

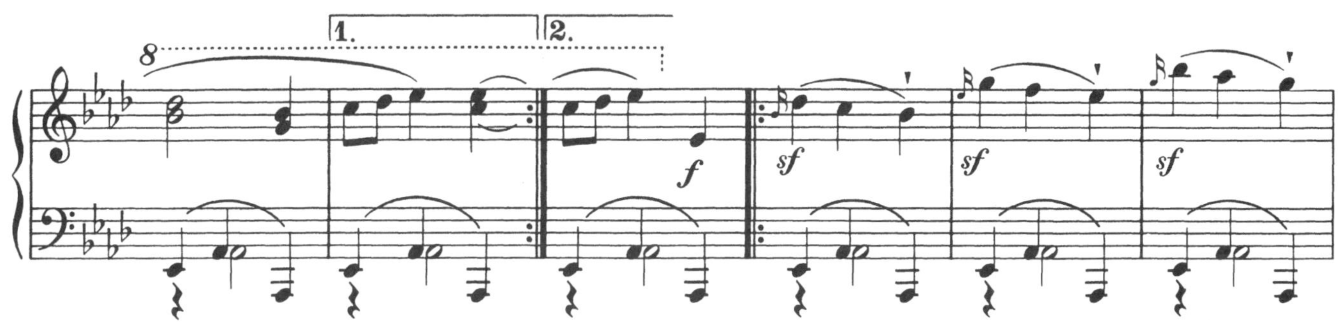

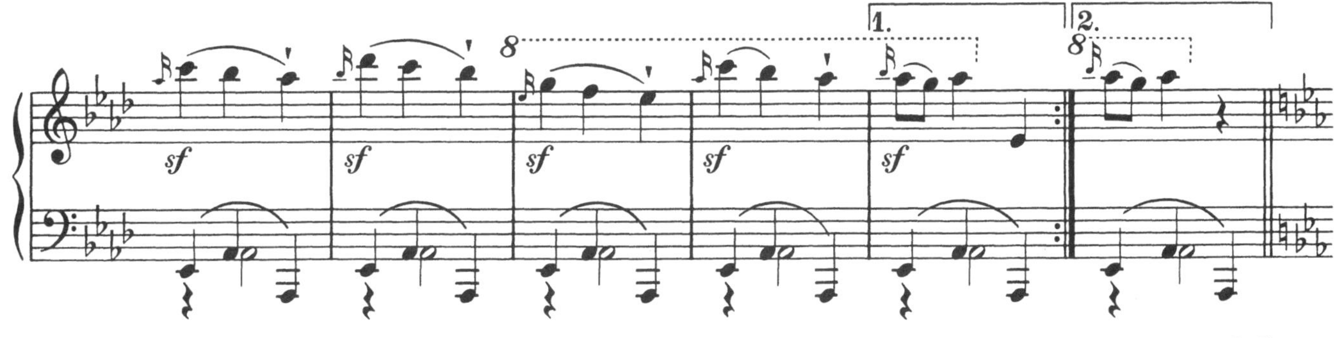

KLAVIERSTÜCK
in G minor

Ludwig van Beethoven
WoO 61a